ISBN 978-0-259-82150-2
PIBN 10827035

1 MONTH OF
FREE
READING

at

www.ForgottenBooks.com

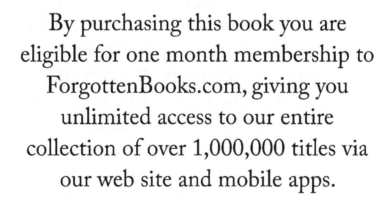

By purchasing this book you are eligible for one month membership to ForgottenBooks.com, giving you unlimited access to our entire collection of over 1,000,000 titles via our web site and mobile apps.

To claim your free month visit:

www.forgottenbooks.com/free827035

English
Français
Deutsche
Italiano
Español
Português

www.forgottenbooks.com

Mythology Photography **Fiction**
Fishing Christianity **Art** Cooking
Essays Buddhism Freemasonry
Medicine **Biology** Music **Ancient**
Egypt Evolution Carpentry Physics
Dance Geology **Mathematics** Fitness
Shakespeare **Folklore** Yoga Marketing
Confidence Immortality Biographies
Poetry **Psychology** Witchcraft
Electronics Chemistry History **Law**
Accounting **Philosophy** Anthropology
Alchemy Drama Quantum Mechanics
Atheism Sexual Health **Ancient History**
Entrepreneurship Languages Sport
Paleontology Needlework Islam
Metaphysics Investment Archaeology
Parenting Statistics Criminology
Motivational

THE VANITY

OF

Earthly Objects of Attachment.

◆·◆·◆

A SERMON,

PREACHED IN ST. ANDREW'S CHURCH, MONTREAL.

ON THE OCCASION OF THE DEATH OF

JAMES HERVEY, Esq.,

BY

ALEXANDER MATHIESON, D.D.

———

(For Private Distribution.)

———

Montreal:
PRINTED BY JOHN LOVELL, ST. NICHOLAS STREET.
1864.

SERMON.

PSALM LXXXVIII. 18.—Lover and friend hast thou put far from me, and mine acquaintance into darkness.

No subject has been more frequently presented to the contemplative mind, or has been the theme of such universal complaint, as the shortness of human life, and the unsatisfactory nature of all our enjoyments. Instability and decay, are stamped upon every thing earthly, and present a strange contrast to the unbounded desires, and flattering hopes of mankind. In his best estate,— on the highest pinnacles of power, of wealth, and grandeur, man is altogether vanity; and not one individual can be selected from the humblest stations in society, who has not at one period of life or another, lamented over blighted hopes and disappointed expectations. "Surely every man walketh in a vain shew." There is nothing substantial, nothing real or permanent in his condition. Even those affections and feelings that are essential elements of our nature.—affections and feelings that shall outlive the fluctuations and changes of mortal life, are, in relation to the objects of time, changeable. The gentle emotions of love, the endearments of friendship, and sympathies of human intercourse, have, in this world, no proper sphere for their exercise or enjoyment. Often in the full flow of the delight which they impart, they are suddenly and unexpectedly terminated, and in the bitterness of disappointed hope is heard the lamentation, "lover and friend, thou hast put far from me, and mine acquaintance into darkness."

Without enquiring into the circumstances, which led the Psalmist to give utterance to those mournful complaints which pervade every part of this sacred song, or adverting to those events in the life and passion of the Redeemer to which they evidently point, we shall in humble dependence on God, make the words which we have selected for our text, the basis of a few observations, on the imperfection of that happiness which results from the exercise of our affections, when they are placed on worldly objects, on the instability of earthly friendships, and the deceitfulness of that trust which is reposed in human wisdom and power; and endeavour to point out some of the lessons which God designs to impress upon the heart of man, through the vanity of temporal enjoyments.

Of all the pleasures that derive their origin exclusively from this world, surely the tender, and mysterious emotions of a holy love, and the endearments of virtuous friendship, are by far the noblest and most satisfactory. Yet these are far from being perfect. The silent, and almost imperceptible changes that are continually passing upon our minds,—the alterations which are constantly occurring in the world around us,—the short duration of our lives, in this precarious state of existence, combine to render all our sublunary joys transient and unsatisfactory. Distance or time may efface the deepest impressions from the heart, an unguarded action, or a rude and inconsiderate expression, may sever in a moment the bonds of friendship. Even that love is chilled by time, which we fondly imagined was stronger than death, and would have survived the withering influences of the grave, and that friendship is no more remembered, which we vainly thought was permanent as the everlasting hills. Other feelings possess the mind; other objects engage the affections, and the passion which once swayed the heart with supreme authority, failing by slow and inperceptible degrees, is at length utterly extinguished. The darkness of oblivion soon hides the past from view, and conceals in its impenetrable shades, those objects that once delighted us: and if not in bitterness of spirit, yet with a feeling of disappointment, we are led to exclaim, "Lover and friend, hast thou put far from me, and mine acquaintance into darkness."

But supposing that our loves and friendships instead of experiencing the slow process of gradual decay, were on the contrary to increase in strength and disinterestedness with the progress of years, yet death would at length put a period to them all; and it might be in an unexpected moment. How often does that destroyer of human happiness, dash from the impatient lip the untasted cup of bliss, and dissipate in the very hour of expected enjoyment, those fair visions of delight which hope has spread before the imagination, and sustained and cherished amidst many disappointments and fears.

But to pass from these general illustrations, which may not come home to your hearts with such a moral force, as those which speak to your individual sympathies, let me request your attention to the exalted happiness which results from domestic love, when sanctified and sublimed by the religion of Christ Jesus. Notwithstanding the cares and anxieties that are mingled with domestic happiness, it is the purest relict of primeval bliss, the brightest emblem on earth of heavenly happiness, or rather, I might say in truth, it is a portion of heaven's happiness, vouchsafed to man here below: for we have at least some reason to believe, that the redeemed shall know in a future state, those who were near and dear unto them on earth, and that those feelings of affection and esteem, which they entertained towards one another, though interrupted, shall not be destroyed by death, but, purified from all that is earthly, shall exist in heaven in undecaying and undisturbed exercise, throughout the ages of eternity.

But pure, elevated, and permanent though such affections are, they are yet,—in so far as they have a relation to this terrestrial state,—interwoven with many sorrows and disappointments. We cannot, while we " tabernacle in houses of clay," soar so far above the world, as to be completely removed from its trials, and its cares. However spiritually minded we may be, these must in some degree affect us. We cannot but feel the disappointments of life, and grieve for the dissolution of those tender ties, which unite us together in this sublunary scene. We cannot so entirely divest ourselves of those associations, which lead us to imagine, that our happiness and protection depend in a great measure on our earthly unions. Yet, often are we doomed, in the inscrutable appointments of providence, to lament the departure of that happiness, which results from the exercise of the holiest feelings of the heart. Can earthly love be more pure, than that which subsists between parents and children, or can dependence be more complete, than that of the infant on parental care ? Even before its eyes are conscious of the light, it seems to look up to the Mother's love, for that support and protection which it needs ; and O with what warmth of affection, and with what tenderness of care, does her answering heart respond to that silent supplication—Or look we to the years of childhood ; that trust is not diminished,—that love is not abated. All the little hopes and fears, the joys and sorrows that affect it, are poured forth with confiding trust, into a bosom that anticipates every wish, and provides for every want.—Or look we to the froward

and impetuous season of youth, when restraint
is apt to be shaken off, and pious advice to be
spurned, we shall yet find there,—unless there
is a deplorable, and an irremediable corruption of
heart,—a deep and reverential respect paid to
parental authority and parental advice; and with
what endurance does the father toil, and with
what anxious care and fervency does the mother
watch and pray for the welfare and guidance of
their offspring. As the surrounding temptations
of life are multiplied, their diligence is redoubled.
Many an anxious hour and sleepless night is
spent in planning their future course in life.
Many a trembling thought, is turned to the dangers
which surround them, or to the hardships to
which they may be exposed in an unfeeling and
sinful world, and thus, when all as it were, seems
to depend on human skill and prudence, and the
continuance of that connection, which is cemented
by mutual love—as if to mock the labours and
expectations of man, suddenly, the fair fabric is
demolished. The child is taken away, and the
parents are left to mourn the extinction of that
love, which made their hearts throb with raptu-
rous delight; or the parents are removed, and the
children are left exposed to all the ills of life,
perhaps it may be without a protector, or a pro-
vider, but that Gracious Being, who hath promised
to protect the fatherless, and who feedeth the
young ravens that cry.

Let us look to another instance of the imperfection of human happiness, resulting from the

mutability of the objects on which we fix our affections.—Let us look to the wedded pair—congeniality of taste and feeling first led to a union, which every year and day made more intimate, and seemed to render more stable. They appear but to live for each others happiness. Their days, checquered only by the little ills that give zest to rational enjoyment, glide away like some delightful dream. Their happiness seems to require little to make it complete, but indefinite duration,—and that, with unfaltering hope they anticipate. Vain hope! Those hearts so firmly united, are torn assunder. The husband is taken away; and the wife, looking on a cold and selfish world with feelings allied to despair, finds not in it, any thing to soothe or comfort her. Or the wife descends into the grave, and the husband is left like a tree stripped of its leaves, and exposed to every storm. Nothing can survive the mutations of time, but the bonds which unite us in feeling and affection, as brethren and friends in Christ Jesus. Nothing else, can resist the corroding rust of age, or triumph over the " King of terrors."

There is no need to advert to individual instances illustrative of these remarks. Into those families where happiness reigned, we often see suddenly introduced sorrow and anguish. The gay visions which prosperity presented to view, are hid by the dark clouds of adversity; and instead of the voice of gladness, or the gentler whispers of peaceful contentment, is heard the voice of weeping, and lamentation, and mourning and woe.

2. Nor are our friendships more stable. They too participate in the mutability and frailty of our nature. Yet, surely of all the pleasures which we are permitted to taste here below, those which spring from virtuous friendship, are among the purest, and bid fairest for perpetuity. We speak not now, of those connections which men often form for their mutual benefit, and are founded entirely on the reciprocal exchange of good offices. It is not to be wondered at, that these should be transient, and that they should disappear, when the causes that produce them are removed. But the friendship that is founded on the best feelings of the human heart, and that is cherished and strengthened by mutual acts of love, is by no means an imaginary blessing. It alleviates sorrow—it soothes anxiety—cheers dejection— and multiplies all the enjoyments of life. Man feeling how much he stands in need of such aid, and how tasteless all the blessings of life are, without a friend to participate in his joy, naturally seeks for one, in whose confiding breast he may with confidence repose his thoughts; and happy is the man who finds one of kindred sentiments, to whom at all times he can impart his joys and sorrows, in the assured hope of sympathy and assistance. No earthly blessing can compensate for the want of a faithful friend. However elevated a man's station may be, or however numerous the train of his dependents may be, he is much to be pitied, who cannot number one at least, among his fellow men, as a true and an attached friend.

It is impossible to enumerate all the advantages of sincere friendship. Many of these are too prominent to be overlooked, even by the most careless observer. But like the modest floweret that lifts its head unseen amidst the flaunting beauties of more conspicuous blossoms, by far the most delightful exercises of friendship, are hid from the gaze of the world. To be known, they must be experienced. There must be a reciprocity of affection and kindness. There must be heart answering to heart—an implicit confidence on one side, and a corresponding fidelity on the other.

Friendships thus formed, have been known to survive the shocks of political strife—to have remained unaltered amidst the vicissitudes of fortune—to have surmounted many discouraging circumstances, fitted to excite suspicion and distrust, and yet have been destroyed at last.

But admitting that no general inference can be deduced from such cases, the disruption of the ties which unite men in friendly union, is not a thing of rare occurance. Even those friendships, that are founded on the best feelings of our nature, have scarcely time amidst the agitations of life, to develop themselves; before they are terminated by death, and perish forever—or linger but for a fleeting season, in the memory of the sad survivors, as things that once have been.

3. Neither is the trust which we repose in the social institutions of mankind, more secure, nor is the happiness derived from such arrangements more permanent, than that which flows from our

loves and friendships. It might be supposed that the imperfections which attach to the exercise of love and friendship, arises in some measure from the selfish nature of these affections—and that were our individual interests more closely connected with the interests of mankind at large, they would possess greater stability, and our happiness derive greater permanency, from the expansion of the principles on which it rests. This however in experience, we will not find to be the case. The leading elements of the social system are not exempted from decay, any more than the ties of friendship or the bonds of love.

There is a social feeling in mankind, that leads them to unite for their mutual benefit and protection. Confederacies of this kind, when founded on just principles, and conducted with integrity, are essential to the peace and happiness of mankind. They inspire the mind with fortitude in the hour of danger. They encourage us in every good work. They enable us to present a more determined resistance to every encroachment on our property, our liberty and lives. In truth, without some degree of confidence in each other, the wheels of life would stand still. Every one would look with a jealous eye on his neighbour, and in the selfishness of his heart, would embrace every opportunity of advancing himself at the expense of another's interests.

To counteract the operation of principles so destructive of human happiness, the beneficient Author of our nature hath endued us with social feelings and affections, and made it a law of his kingdom, that we shall derive a great proportion of our happiness from their exercise. Even where they are not so concentrated, as to constitute that state of mind which is properly denominated love, or friendship, they are highly favorable both to our security and comfort; and the happiness and improvement of the human condition, seems to correspond with the number and efficiency of our social institutions. One of the purposes for which the ever blessed Son of God came into the world, was, by elevating and purifying the elementary principles of these institutions, to set them on a more solid and permanent basis, and free them from that selfishness, which would retard and destroy their beneficial operations.

It is therefore perfectly consistent with the will of God, that we place a certain degree of confidence in each other., But the danger ; is that we put our undivided trust in an arm of flesh. We are often reminded of the frailty of such supports.--- Often warned to " cease from man whose breath is in his nostrils." But instead of putting our trust in God, and looking to man as the, instrument only, by which he effects his purposes, we are apt to regard the presence of those, on whom under God—we have been dependent, as essentially connected with our happiness. No one who is acquainted with the state of his own heart, or who casts a glance at the pursuits of men—will deny, that there is a fearful tendency in the human heart, to forget God. That there is a

cherished enmity there, which would thrust him
from the throne of his empire, and exclude him
from the government of the world, which he has
made for the manifestation of his glory. Do we
not often find men, in utter defiance of the re-
quisitions of God's law, form their worldly schemes,
and in utter disregard of its threatenings, prosecute them with all their heart and with all their
mind? Do they not in the exercise of their pre-
scribed social duties overlook his agency, and cast
off all dependence on him? Do they not in the
enjoyment of his bounties, fail to recognize his
beneficence, and ascribe their success to the
strength of their own arm, and the well-directed
energies of their own mind? And do they not,
when the comforts of life are wrested from them,
grieve for their loss, in a way that plainly indi-
cates their hearts were set upon these things, and
not upon God, as the well-spring of their blessedness. And that they distrust his power to protect
them—and his wisdom to provide for them, in-
dependently of those sublunary protectors of
which they have been deprived. And wonderful
it is; that all this is felt and done, amidst hourly
demonstrations of the vanity of those objects on
which we lean for our happiness. How often do
we see the destinies of a nation suspended on the
life of a single individual. He is taken away—
the political atmosphere is changed—and all that
seemed permanent and prosperous in the national
policy is scattered to the winds. How often are
the interests of a mercantile community, in a

great measure involved in the successful projects of a few enterprising men. They are removed from the busy scenes of life,—commerce seeks another channel, or for a time, languishes in a more sluggish stream. How often does the success of individuals, and the comfort of families seem to depend on the continued energies of one lofty intellect, or on the tender care of one watchful Guardian. Death unexpectedly terminates the connection. They who have lived in affluence; are obliged to descend into the vale of humble life, with their trust in God alone, whose mercy faileth never. They who have been tended with more than a parent's love; are left to the care of strangers, with no other hope but that which springs from the promises of Him who spreads his sheltering wings over the destitute and forlorn.

Nothing can support the soul amidst the mutations and sorrows of life, but the faith, that the unchangeable God is a " present help in the day of trouble." This is a refuge always open to the believer. He can look beyond all that is distressing or unsatisfactory in his earth-born joys, and draw his happiness from a pure and never failing fountain.

Though the separations of life, are, and cannot but be painful to the children of mortality, compelling them in bitterness of spirit to exclaim, " lover and friend hast thou put far from me, and mine acquaintance into darkness:" yet the gracious purposes of God are thereby most wonderfully accomplished. A moment's reflection might

convince us, that whatsoever conduces to call off
our affections from the objects which withdraw
our hearts from God, and concentrate them
on him, is a merciful dispensation.—That whatsoever relieves us from the burdens of life, and
introduces us to the happiness that is at God's
right hand, is a most desirable appointment. It
may present a different aspect to us. It may
come in a moment when we looked not for it.
It may wear the attributes of divine indignation;
and appalled and desponding we may exclaim,
" hath God forgotten to be gracious, and will he
be favourable no more; hath he shut up in anger
his tender mercies, and doth his promise fail for
evermore." But, as when the blackness of the
storm has somewhat passed away, and the sun
begins to break through the dark impending
clouds, revealing the long parched earth, begin-
ning to smile in renewed freshness and beauty;
so when the first gush of sorrow is passed, our
afflictions,—if they are received in meek submis-
sion to the will of God, and sanctified by the
grace of the Redeemer—viewed in connection with
their ultimate effects upon our principles and con-
duct, will appear the most expressive tokens of
God's tenderest love for our souls. In their
blessed results we will have much reason to be
thankful, that rather than we should be left at a
distance from God, and to seek for our happiness
in objects which cannot bestow perfect or permanent felicity, we should be subjected to the seve-
rest trials, and those objects on which our hopes

and joys were centred should be taken away from us, or the message sent to ourselves, " Arise ye, and depart. This is not your rest; because it is polluted, it will destroy you with a sore destruction."

It is only as pilgrims through this valley of tears that we have cause to mourn over the bereavements of life. It is only, in so far as our affections are interwoven with the objects and events of time; that we are destined to lament that " lover and friend have been put far from us." That state of mind which constitutes love, or friendship, or philanthropy, has in reality nothing in common with the materialities of the world. These feelings are of a spiritual nature, and cannot be essentially affected by the mutations of material things. They flow from the intercommunings of soul with soul,—intercommunings that are indeed maintained on earth, through the medium of things that are seen and tangible, but they are distinct from these things. Death may suspend their action, but it cannot destroy the sentiments themselves. They are spiritual, and over *them* death has no power. The very strength and constancy of true love and virtuous friendship plainly indicate, that they have not their origin in time, and that they shall survive " the wreck of nature." Transferred to a region where everything is pure and permanent, they shall have full scope for their exercise, and forever " flourish in immortal youth." It is only the links that connect them with the things of time that can be broken. The heavenly qualities that evoke these sentiments; perish never.

Viewing the several trials of life from this stand point, how kind and gracious do they appear. Surely it is in "very mercifulness, God afflicts us." By destroying the elements of our affections which are earthly, and separating what is mortal, from what is spiritual, God gives to the holy feelings,—which in a subordinate degree, we are permitted to rest on material objects,—imperishable objects to rest upon. By giving the objects of our love and friendship, immortality, he makes them, in some measure commensurate to the capacities and desires of our immortal souls—he elevates the happiness which flows from the exercise of the holy affections of our nature, above the troubles and vicissitudes of this fleeting world, and establishes a permanent connection between our souls, and the dear objects of which death has bereaved us. Death does not destroy the spiritual intercourse that subsists between relatives and friends—it only destroys *that* which is earthly; it leaves untouched *that* which is heavenly. The ties that bind the parent and child—the husband and wife—the brother, the sister and friend, are spiritual, and indissoluble— and freed from their earthly element, shall exist, when the world and the things of the world shall have passed away forever.

To the believer in Christ Jesus, what unspeakable consolation does the reflection afford, that when separated from his beloved friends, it is only a temporary interruption of holy affection, for which he has to mourn. Or I should rather say,—he has only to grieve for the departure of the visible form; for there still subsists a myste_ rions intercourse between the soul, and the spirits of his departed friends in Christ. They are all members of the same family—having the same Father—and under the same gracious care. " Ye are come" says the apostle Paul, " unto Mount Zion and to the city of the living God, the heavenly Jerusalem, and to an innumerable company of angels. To the general assembly and church of the first born, which are written in heaven. And to God the judge of all, and to the spirits of just men made perfect, and to Jesus the Mediator of the new covenant, and to the blood of sprinkling that speaketh better things than the blood of Abel."

Nothing is so well calculated to comfort and console the mind, under the bereavements of life, than the conviction, that they, who have been removed from the manifestations of their love, and the expressions of their friendship, are gone to enjoy in its ineffable fulness, the love and friendship of the Redeemer. He loves them more intensely than we possibly can; he gives them to enjoy a happiness more elevated and pure, than could possibly spring from the exercise of our tenderest affections. This consolation is the " sure portion" of all those who have resigned, in faith and hope, their believing friends into the hands of the God of love. In the view opened

up to the mind of the Christian, by the Gospel;
time and space are annihilated. The keen eye of
faith reaches far into eternity—the soul, forget-
ting the earthly medium of communication, and
asserting its birth-right privilege, enters into the
spiritual world, to hold communings with those
who are around the throne of the Most High, and
to participate in some degree of their joy. If
they cannot while they are in the body always
remain in a state of spiritual abstraction—yet,
when they descend to the duties and cares of the
world, like the face of Moses, which shone with
resplendent lustre, when he descended from the
nount of communion with God, their faces will
shine as it were, with the radiance of heaven.
Their minds will be more spiritual, their affections
more pure. Their expressions of regard for their
families and friends will not be limited by this
world's happiness—but ranging through the infin-
ite expanse of blessedness, shed on them through
the love of God in Christ Jesus, they will earnestly
implore that the riches of heaven's gifts will be
bestowed upon them. With respect to those who
have gone before them into glory, they will be
heard no longer to exclaim, " Lover and friend
hast thou put far from me, and mine acquaintance
into darkness,"—but rather,—" Blessed be the
God and Father of our Lord Jesus Christ, the
Father of Mercies, that he hath translated them
from a land of darkness and death, unto a land
of unclouded light and everlasting life."
The lessons which our text inculcates are

numerous and important. To one or two of these, let me call your attention.

1. It admonishes us, not to place our affections on the things of this world, since every thing in it, apart from God, is insufficient to confer on us true happiness. The blessings of Providence are gifts from God. When we receive them with thankful hearts, and endeavour to apply them to the purposes for which they were given us, they become instruments in his hands of the highest importance, for elevating and improving our moral nature. They are not only encouraging assurances of divine love, but they also animate us to prosecute with diligence the "things of our peace." They increase our desires for perfect and enduring happiness;—at the same time, that their unsatisfying nature and precarious enjoyment, prevents us from lingering here, while unmingled happiness awaits us hereafter. Even in the height of their enjoyment, we readily enter into the spirit of the Patriarch, when he exclaimed, "I would not live always."—"O that I had the wings of a dove, that I might flee away and be at rest."

But instead of making our temporal blessings subservient to our spiritual progress, too often, when they are multiplied, we set our hearts upon them, and not upon God, as the well-spring of blessedness. More especially, if they come to us through the channels of human love and friendship. These agencies become so associated with our happiness, that, if they are removed, we

distrust the goodness and Almighty power of God
to comfort or protect us.

2. We are taught by our bereavements that
the Almighty designs to draw off all undue attach-
ment to the things of sense and of time, that our
trust may be placed upon himself, the fountain
of all true blessedness. Implicit trust in God,
is one of the most exalted, yet one of the most
difficult exercises of religion—difficult!—not
because we are unwilling to acknowledge his per-
fections; but O it is a hard thing, to make us
renounce all dependence upon ourselves, and those
who are disposed to befriend us, and cast ourselves
implicitly on his care, both for the things of this
world and the next. This is a lesson that our
sinful hearts can only learn in the gloom of sorrow
and affliction. We must feel the vanity of those
things on which we are so apt to repose our confidence, before we can practically acknowledge,
that in God alone our rest is to be found, and
that in vain would we seek for repose apart from
him.

3. We are taught, that the Almighty designs
to give full scope to the exercise of those holy
feelings and affections of our nature, by giving
immortality to the objects on which they rest.
The happiness that results from the exercise of
our sanctified affections, however elevated, is yet
from the frailty of the objects on which they are
fixed, far from being perfect. Disappointments,
mar our earth-born joys. Death, terminates them
for ever. What we want to make our happiness

complete, is permanency—is freedom from death —is life—eternal life! The only way that we can acquire this element of true felicity is through faith in Christ. "He is the *way*, the *truth* and the *life*." "Whosoever liveth and believeth in *Me*," said he, "shall never die." To obtain this life, we must go to *Him*—we must follow him into the darkness of death. "The body cannot be quickened unless it die,"—but through the process of dissolution our natural bodies are made spiritual bodies, fitted for an endless life.

Such, my friends, are some of the gracious purposes which God has in view; when he sends severe afflictions to his people. Thus he reminds them, that here, they have no resting place—that here, they can expect no solid or permanent delight—that their home is in a better world—and that to enjoy its comforts and happiness, he prepares them by making them pass through great tribulations. The events of providence come to illustrate and enforce the truths, which the scriptures reveal concerning an endless life. And O how impressively they teach us—if our minds are capable of receiving serious instructions—the necessity for making due preparation for an eternal world. They have often uttered their warning voice of preparation in our ears. May God give us grace, not to receive their intimations in vain. They will soon carry the message to each one of us "the time of your departure is at hand—this is not your rest. Arise ye and depart unto the rest which the Lord God giveth you." And may God grant that an abundant entrance may be administered unto us all into his presence in glory.

A sadder illustration of our text seldom occurs, than what has brought mourning and sorrow to many a heart, by the sudden removal by death, of one of the members of this congregation.* It was but last Lord's day we found him in his customary place among us, a devout worshipper of the living God. Since that time—short as it has been,—we have laid his body in the dust. His spirit has gone to God who gave it; and we are not left without "the well-grounded hope" that through the merits of his Redeemer, in whom his hope and confidence were placed; it now mingles with "the spirits of just men made perfect" around the throne on high.

It has not been my custom—as you are aware—specially to advert to the death of individual worshippers among you—or even, except in a very general way, to enforce the lessons of the uncertainty of human happiness, which incidents unexpected and sad may give us. But the suddenness of this event,—the sorrow it has struck into the hearts of so many who looked to him as a father and a friend—and who now mourn his departure, giving utterance to their emotions in the expressive language of the text, may warrant me to crave for a moment your attention, while, on this solemn occasion, I advert to a few characteristic traits of that generous hearted man—

* James Hervey, Esq.

and it may be, that after an unbroken friendship of more than half a century, I may be permitted to mingle my plaints with the deeper wailings of their sorrows. Unselfish, kind, and affectionate, he bound to him the hearts of his family, with a tie almost too strong; wherewith to be bound to any object of earthly affection, consistently with a supreme regard to Him, to whom we can alone look with confidence as our Protector and "the Giver of every good and perfect gift." His heart, flowing with human sympathies, attracted the fond love of his relatives, and secured the lasting esteem of his friends, while he was ever ready to relieve the distresses of his fellow creatures, of whatever country or religious profession they might be. Nor were his acts of kindness the mere impulses of a generous nature. They were based on Christian principles—they sprung from sincere piety—from love to God and love to men. His piety was rational, eminently practical, habitual and cheerful, manifested in a dutiful observance of religious ordinances—in a tender attention to the spiritual progress and temporal exigencies of those dependent upon him,—in the integrity of his transactions—and in the last moments of his life, in his sincere and humble trust in the mercy of God, his Saviour. Reviewing his past life, he confessed his utter unworthiness of God's manifold mercies, and expressed his thankfulness for the afflictions which he sent, assured that it was good for him to be afflicted.

Though suddenly cut down, with a disease that

generally prostrates every mental faculty as well
as every physical energy, God was mercifully
pleased to preserve his consciousness almost to the
last moment. After giving a few directions relative to the settlement of his worldly affairs, he
turned his mind to his solemn position before
God. The concentration of his thoughts on the
great truths of religion was remarkable; and the
fervency with which he poured out his heart in
prayer, has left with his sorrowing friends a token
of his firm faith in Christ Jesus, to console them,
amidst their fond—but sorrowful remembrances,
and stir them up to secure the same comforting
hopes for their dying hour. "I know that my
Redeemer liveth." "Christ is my only hope, my
all in all." "Into thy hands I commend my
spirit, Lord God of Truth, thou hast redeemed
me," were a few of the devout exclamations he
uttered in his last moments.

On the last Sabbath evening, as was his custom,
he assembled the several members of his house-
hold; and the lessons drawn from the instructions
which they had heard that day within the house
of God, were,—I have been informed,—peculiarly
earnest and impressive, confirmed as they have
been by the solemnities of his last moments. May
they make a deep and lasting impression on the
minds of all who heard them, to the praise and
glory of God. Amen.

CPSIA information can be obtained
at www.ICGtesting.com
Printed in the USA
BVHW041130161218
535629BV00038B/1267/P